I SEE,
I THINK,
I BECOME

A Collection of Poetry

I SEE,
I THINK,
I BECOME

A Collection of Poetry

LADY V MADISYN

I SEE, I THINK, I BECOME
A Collection of Poetry

Copyright © 2021 Lady V Madisyn

Illustrated by: Elmira Georgieva

Printed in the United States of America

ISBN: 978-1-64484-316-1 (print)
ISBN: 978-1-64484-317-8 (ebook)

Special discounts are available on bulk quantity purchases by book clubs, associations and special interest groups. For details email: belove128llc@gmail.com or call (888) 949-6228.

For information log on to www.belovellc.com

To my Grammy, Louise B. H. O'Daniel

CONTENTS

Author Message To The Reader

*May the love of God be the
beacon that abides in the
heart. May peace dwell
within, and the joy of the
Lord manifest compassion
and patience to guide
humanity, always abiding in
love for self and others as remnants
of woven unity. Beloved, believe, conceive, receive your ancestry is a
bloodline filled with a rich heritage that creates legacy. Family is family,
so love, respect, and protect the unbreakable lifetime blood bond. Envision
purpose through introspective lenses, for what is seen enables thinking,
often critical to seize it, and to become it. Man, woman, boy, or girl,
transform your heart and mind.
See it. Think it. Become it.
Bridge love relationships to
build the kingdom and
bestow your gifts from the
heart in truth. Family
is, The Crown Jewel!
#AmericaComeTogether!
#Family! #Love! #Peace!
#ISeeIThinkIBecome!*

I SEE, I THINK, I BECOME

Absorb, like a sponge, my eyes,
I see, people,
Translated,
To the brain,
I think, environment,
Transferred,
Everything Jake?
Careful, economic, political, social views,
God searches the heart. Now, Faith! Free will.
I become, action,
Do you know your worth?
Make a move. Choose.
The Heart is seen, truth or lie.
No. It's not a feeling.
It's a sense, recognize Spirit, search the soul,
Renew. Be ye, transform the mind.
Epiphany, aha!
Introspect connects the core.
An idiosyncratic release.
Now,
I See, I Think, I Become!

Reflections

PEACE

Eyes open to the core. No fear.
See!
The mind is a bridge to the soul.
What? Careful,
I see you.
A mind overtaken, recalling snapshots,
Release. Reflect. Reveal,
A living soul, life moments in time.
What do you see?
Thoughts embedded in the brain.
Day by day,
Accept, forgive, laugh, smile, love,
The core is connected to the soul.
Renew, exude light!
Forward movement, press, create, write,
Life is a story.
Some say a blueprint.
What do you see?
Transparent, blue sky.
Harmony flows with possibility,
Ease, amity, camaraderie, eminence.
Imagine,
I've already become you.
Think!

Inform. Enlighten. Teach.
The core transforms the mind.
Now, you want to draw a weapon,
Ouch!
Hot metal,
Six feet underground.
Careful. The core transforms the mind.
Look inside, eyes reveal the heart,
Now,
Become!
What do you see?
Release. Reflect. Reveal,
Educate to elevate.
Imprints,
Envisioned,
Surrender,
Trust,
The Spirit lives within.
Promote * Elevate * Achieve * Create * Excellence
PEACE!

Reflections

MY GOD, THE LIFE, I CHOOSE

God is,
I AM.
Sovereign,
Author, finisher, truth,
A living Spirit!
Breathe, press forward,
Choose Life.
Yesterday, it's gone,
It holds no wind.
Today, I hurt really bad,
They say, you see it, seize it.
Abound.
Hope!
Choose Life.
Stand still,
Connect with the architect.
God tell me how to move forward,
Stand still,
Find your voice.
The Word!
Power!
Choose Life.
The Blood!

Speak.
Holy Ghost!
Good, God Almighty!
Now, Faith.
His yoke is easy,
Burden's light,
Man, Woman, Boy, Girl,
Living soul,
Surrender.
Choose Life!

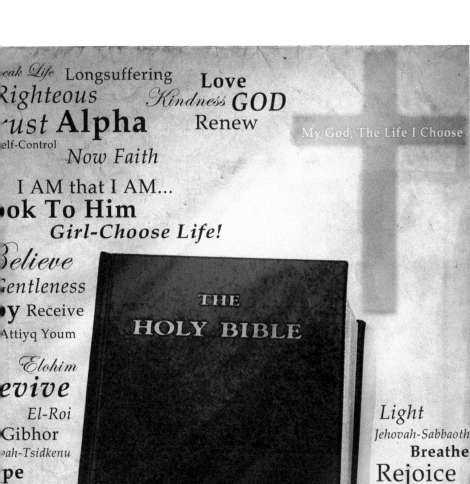

eak Life Longsuffering **Love**
Righteous *Kindness* **GOD**
ust **Alpha** Renew
elf-Control

Now Faith

I AM that I AM...
ok To Him
Girl-Choose Life!

Believe

Gentleness

y Receive

Attiyq Youm

Elohim

evive

El-Roi

Gibhor

ah-Tsidkenu

pe

My God, The Life I Choose

THE HOLY BIBLE

Light
Jehovah-Sabbaoth
Breathe
Rejoice
El-Olam

Yahweh
Jehovah-Jireh
Survive

Fruits of the Spirit

Jehovah-Rapha

Jehovah-Ghmolah Just

El-Chuwl *Thrive*

El-Deah Jehovah-Rohi

Life *El-Shaddai-Rohi*

Jehovah-Nissi **Omega**

Jehovah - Shalom

Jehovah-Maccaddeshem

Jehovah-Shammah Adonai

Goodness El-Elyon

Conceive

Reflections

THE BLACK MAN

Who is you? What's your blueprint?
King, patriarch, my brother,
A keeper. Truth be told.
Now, endangered, hunted, broken,
No equal justice,
Uh oh, buried in the ground.
Say it ain't so, truth be told.
Who is you? What's your blueprint?
Say it!
Athlete, entertainer, politician, preacher,
You know your position.
Privileged?
Green paper stacked so nice,
Daddy, bae, sweetheart, big poppa.
Look, you know your name,
Who is you? What's your blueprint?
You pay my bills so good,
Power!
Sex!
Money!
Control, it's a money game.
Checkers or chess?
Oh, honey, you know I love you,
See!

There it is, your blueprint.
A Black Man story.
You ask,
Who is you? What's your blueprint?
Black Man, born to Isms,
Beaten, choked, broken, battered into the ground.
Screaming, my God, how the hell do I cope?
Damn, I need money to survive,
I got melanin in my skin.
Hold up, wait a minute. Almighty?
Hell no, it's Lucifer, you can't cancel me.
God allows.
Now, engulfed into the sea of forgetfulness,
Negative, horrible, heinous, horrific, weak, coward.
Eradicated, cast out, unseen,
Bad actor no more, you can't cancel me.
God allows.
The Black Man is pious, worthy, righteous, just,
A purposed man of Faith,
Family head,
Core of strength.
He loves, has courage,
Resilient, leads, creates.
The Black Man is ancestry, legacy, a blood line.
Who is he? What's his blueprint?
The Black Man is a winner,
Say it, that is his name.

Not characterized or dehumanized
By melanin shades.
His character embodies keys to surrender,
Forgiveness to build bridges,
Freewill to choose love.
Just, right, not delayed, nor denied,
Introspective ownership, provides, covers,
Protects his Seed.
Grows, understands, teaches,
Walks what he talks,
The Word.
God is,
A Savior.
The Black Man presses forward,
Achieves life goals,
Prepares, strives, abundantly thrives,
No matter the cause.
Believes, receives,
I am a Man.
Now, arise!
See,
Think,
Become,
A King!

Da
Son
FRIEND
Husband
DAD Uncle
Teacher **Father**
FUNNY *Brother* Papa
Pops *Provider*
Courage Strength
LOVE **Strong** *Legacy*
TREND STARTER
Creative *Bright*
INNOVATOR **Melanin**
Brilliant *Heritage*
WONDROUS *Resilience*
Beautiful *Patriarch*
Worthy **Forefather**
Leader ARCHITECT
cool *Inventor* **Smart**
Daddy **Entrepreneur**
Wisdom Bloodline
ELDER *Ancestors*
Covers CHARISMA
Preacher **Blueprint**

The Black Man

Character Minister
WINNER
Lady V Mae

Reflections

GRAMMY DROPPING SEEDS

Cathy...

And, when she called me Cathy, Grammy Louise would say I want you to always remember, to thine own self be true. Early shared wisdom, seeds dropped, they call it life advice. She'd say to understand your purpose in life can be a painful struggle. But it can also be a soft, sweet, aromatic scent like a fragrance after the rain. Can you see it?

A blossomed rose in a field of lavender greens. Listen, feel your heart thumping. Got to fill that void. Bring forth the vision. Find your voice. Life can be an unfruitful journey, connected to bad roots, un-watered love, in search of love, plagued with dark hills that don't glisten in due season.

Cathy, that's what we call lust, baby. A life paralyzed in fear no hope, wavered faith, a schematic fit unseen. You've got to look toward God. Learn how to pray. Trust in Him. Store it up Faith. She'd say remember, life can be an unfruitful journey. Then, is the time to dig deep, speak it, believe it, receive it. Now that's what we call cashing in life seeds of Faith. Walk it. You are victorious!

Shugee...

Shugee! She'd say understand this. It really doesn't matter how long you have known him. A key to the heart is that a man recognizes that there is an inner connection. A magnetic bond that draws you into his heart. A man covers a woman.

I'll tell it to you like this, what the eyes see influences the heart, and just like planted seeds, now the man becomes what he envisions and believes from the heart. Think about it. Whether it is in three seconds, minutes, hours, days, weeks, months, years, or decades, a keeper's heart knows within his lifetime when he has found, The One!

Babygirl...

Babygirl! You hear me? Sex is a wonderful thing. But you have got to have more in common than sex. Why? Because it gets old as a funky hard rag. Be clear, that's why it is always better letting go and releasing with that special one who really means something. You see it, think, understand, the heart knows, then it releases. Truth be told, you have met this kind before. Sex, the hot scent to a sensual allure as when the eyes meet to become one, and the warmth of flesh intertwines, and pimples with goosebumps. The sounds of pillow screams for a closer seamless fit, lit with an on-fire connection that weakens the stomach like butterflies.

Yep, let loose. You give me butterflies baby. An aromatic ooze of adrenaline traveling throughout the body. Straightway to the head, then that soft pulsating calmness flows into a feeling of light airy clouds. But! You have got to have more in common than sex. You listening to me? It's just your old Grammy talking, hmm. Hell naw! It's called wisdom baby. Head up, back straight at my table, Babygirl! Grammy dropping seeds. Now, let's prepare for the harvest.

Reflections

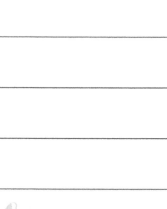

LOVE HARD

A ring,
Tightly woven,
Spun, poured,
An unbreakable bond.
Bed of truth,
No lies between us.
Rhythmic beat,
Inner thighs curved,
Shaped to my emotions.
Love Hard.
No breaks.
Beautiful brown eyes,
Open windows to my heart.
His lips,
Her lips,
Our lips.
Deeply rooted,
Press forward,
Move those hips.
Love Hard.
No breaks.
Release power.
Godlike Faith!

Armor,
Tightly woven. Speak it,
Think positive,
Take action,
Press!
Fight the good fight,
Release power.
Now, that's fire!
Godlike Faith!
It's okay,
Surrender,
Embrace,
Love Hard!

Reflections

_____

_____

_____

_____

_____

_____

_____

_____

_____

_____

_____

BUTTERFLIES

Butterflies.
Wings spread wide, mesmerizing,
Beautiful, bright, boldly flowing,
Love fills the air, as two become one.
I see your brown eyes, I breathe your air,
Infused moments in time, up close,
Colorful, sensing through waterfalls.
Butterflies.
Wings spread wide, mesmerizing,
Flowing, round and round,
There you are, gently,
Release, I taste your sweet kisses.
One finger, slowly,
Moving across the bottom lip, careful now.
No, it's just butterflies,
Feel me, inside a warm rush.
Butterflies.
Wings spread wide, mesmerizing,
A pulsating hot flush.
Red cheeks, now soaring off my feet.
Oh honey, my sweet, sweet, sweet baby,
Toes wiggling, rhythmic heartbeats in sync.
Fruitful, multiply, replenish in season.
Butterflies.
Wings spread wide, mesmerizing,
Limitless love.
Release.
Soar! Soar! Soar!

Butterflies

Lady V Mac

Reflections

AN ANGEL

Don't, look down at me,
Unless you can lift me up!
I see you, Nose turned up.
Who are you? You're not lit.
Don't, look down at me,
Unless you can lift me up!
Guess who's watching?
Oh, my God!
An Angel,
But you're not real.
Don't, look down at me,
Unless you can lift me up!
Is this a test?
You tell me.
Oh, my God!
An Angel,
Oh, my God!
Assigned, and girded around Me!
Beloved,
A sweet-smelling savor!
Receive it!
Conceive it!
Believe it!
Don't, look down at me,
Unless you can lift me up!
Watch!
Be careful,
You've just entertained, *An Angel.*

Reflections

YOU A DREAMER

Uh oh,
You are a Dreamer!
Say what!
You talking to me?
You are a Dreamer!
Say what!
You talking to me?
You are a Dreamer!
Okay.
I Think,
Limitless. Peace. Success.
I Believe,
Liberty. Prosperity. Spirit.
I Conceive,
Love. Purpose. Stability.
I Receive,
Life. Power. Soundness.
By Faith, I sense,
A dreamer, dreams, dreams.
Live. Prepare. Stand.
Put your shoes on,
Press forward,
Manifest your destiny.

Reflections

MY FRIEND

Unselfish love,
You are my friend.
I raise my left hand, examine it closely,
It's an extension of me.
As we touch, it mirrors your right hand.
You feel my pain. I bear your cross.
Silly laughs, deep discussions,
My friend.
We admit anger, release fear,
Let it go,
No grudges. No worries.
My friend.
We take long walks,
Release weights of this world,
Negativity cast out,
Forgive,
My friend.
Serene, like the great falls of water,
Liberally flowing through the palms of my hands,
Transparent, clear, honest, true,
My friend.
Heartfelt to the core, you understand,
My infirmities, high expressed emotions,
Are not meant for gossip,
My friend.
I taste your tears.
You bear my pain.

My friend.
An unbreakable blood bond,
Tree rooted, tightly knit,
Woven unity,
Circling within a tapestry of love,
My friend.
Together, we share a pod,
In sync,
A rhythmic heartbeat,
Shalom,
My friend.
A familiar sound,
Forget about it.
Let's keep it moving.
I just said that. Same thing.
We agree to disagree.
I am your friend.
You are my friend.
Beloved, even in silence,
We find compassion to love.
Rhythmic heart beats become one.
We breathe the same air,
In and out of seasons,
Until,
His work is done,
My friend.
May heaven smile upon you always . . .

Reflections

KEEP IT REAL, WITH MY GOD

God searches the heart,
Believer,
Keep it real.
Today is a new day,
Righteous,
Just,
Compassion,
Work, get it done.
Your season, judgment leveled.
The Word pricks the heart,
It's real.
The Word.
Prepare.
Now!
Keep it real.
Your Weapon,
The Word.
Leader, serve,
Void not,
The Word is Now,
Conceive, believe, receive.
Keep It Real With My God.

43

Reflections

DREAM YOUR DREAM, SPEAK IT!

Dream,
Manifest the vision!
See it!
Embedded in the core.
Think it!
Dream Your Dream,
Speak it!
Captured in the heart.
Oh, but to dream. I become it,
A beautiful burst of sunshine.
Gliding effortlessly,
The sky is filled with transparent pillows.
I hear the wind.
I see light blue skies,
Five feet high, seven foot wide,
Across the miles, north, east, south, west,
Dream Your Dream,
Speak it!
In and out of season,
Red, green, yellow, orange, brown crinkly leaves.
Wind sounds of autumn, winter, spring, summer, fall,
A colorful tapestry of love fills the air.
Seated at the feet of wisdom,

I am told,
Timeless,
Infinite possibilities.
Go get it,
Dream Your Dream,
Speak it!
A heavenly vision conceived from above,
Release the power,
Plead the blood.
Faith,
Hope,
Joy,
Love,
Peace,
Walk into it.
Dream Your Dream,
Speak it!

Dream Your Dream ... Speak it

Blood
PROSPERITY
Sunshine   Truth   HOPE   Speak
LOVE   Imagine
iding   Praise   Blue Skies
mises of God   MANIFEST
e Vision   Tapestry   Peace
Realized   FAITH   The Core
Power

V. Madisyn

Reflections

SCARED MONEY
DON'T MAKE NO MONEY

Plant the seed,
Soil meets a river of waters,
Now, let it grow.
What are you afraid of?
Fear not, firmly rooted.
Always running, back peddling,
Drowning in a tunnel of fear,
You got good roots,
Let it grow.
Unbelief,
Rapidly losing your lease on life,
Wake up!
You see it, get lit,
Fear not,
Scared money is not your friend.
Beloved, trust and believe.
Seeds of wisdom,
Planted, envision, speak,
Think, the tongue is power,
Now, it's harvest time.
Life!
Light!
Love!
Hypocrite,
Release your fears.

You are salt of the earth.
Imagine,
Manifest your dreams.
Light of the world,
A believer,
A chosen generation,
It's your season,
Rooted to become,
Release confidence,
Fear not,
Scared money is not your friend.
Decree it!
Speak it!
Believe it!
Receive it!
The battle is in your mind,
God is,
Spirit, not seen.
Money, sex, power,
Remember,
Scared Money Don't Make No Money.
Be bold,
Walk into your destiny.

Faith

The Mind

ivers of Water

Harvest

Attraction

Believe

Declare

Seeds

Scared Money Don't Make No Money

Growth

Rooted

Seize It

Fruit

See

Wisdom

Battle

Time

Become

Legacy

Think

Seductive

Speak

Receive

Lady V Madisyn

Reflections

A TAPESTRY OF WOVEN UNITY

My colors are your colors,
Reach out, touch my hands.
My colors are your colors,
In the mirror,
Look deeply at my hands.
Woven uniquely,
My colors are meant to understand.
My colors are your colors,
Listen closely,
Strike a balance,
Touch, feel,
Connect with my hands,
You, understand.
A woven tapestry.
My colors are your colors,
A tapestry of woven unity,
Colors blended within thee.
Lifting up, pulling, pushing,
Piercing through,
Don't let go.
Hold on.
Stop!
My colors are your colors,
There is a light!

Yes, you know my colors,
Reach out touch my hands.
My colors are your colors,
A tapestry of woven unity,
I am you,
You are me.
A collection,
A community,
A constellation,
One voice.
Powerful!
Timeless,
Our strength transcends,
You and me,
Colors of Woven Unity!

Reflections

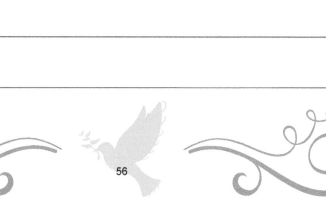

DRUNK, DON'T DRIVE!

Drinking, drinking, drinking,
Loud, speeding, excessive laughter,
Out of control.
Don't do it,
Sober up!
Drunk, driving.
Listening to music,
Mock speed, weaving,
Distracted, yep, and still driving.
Drunk, driving.
Uh oh, look,
Driver out of control.
Driving, drunk,
Now checking,
Where's my mirror,
Gotta keep a beat face,
Diva!
Flawless,
Sweet smelling and fresh.
Car windows down,
Dude, your music, too loud.
Driver out of control.

One hand on the wheel,
Distracted, not thinking,
Drinking, drinking, drinking.
Diva!
Dude!
Drunk on power,
They say nobody knows,
We've done it plenty times before.
Uh oh,
No, no, no!
Too late.
Crashed, flipped, twisted.
Oh my God!
Cars over a bridge.
Explosion, climbing miles,
Oh my God!
A mother,
Newborn babies caught in a burning bush.
The camera flicks,
The police, yellow tape in place.
Driver out of control.
Diva!
Dude!
See what happens,
Drunk while driving,
Sober up!

Listen,

See   Think   Become

Power   Control

ake up   Safety First

DRUNK DON'T DRIVE

Dude   Diva

Sober Up!

Lady V Madisyn

Reflections

_____

_____

_____

_____

_____

_____

_____

_____

_____

_____

_____

_____

YOUR MOMMA!

A powerful Spirit.
Your Momma,
A gift from God.
A force of life.
Destiny to serve.
A birthing vessel.
Deliver,
Breath of life,
Now a living soul.
Original,
Source.
Identification,
Mother.
Purpose,
Significant.
Compelling,
Matriarch.
Nurturer,
Her strength.
Backbone,
Style.
Family legacy.
Call her,
Mimi, Mum, Mama,
Mammy, Maem, Mom,

Ma, Lightning, Madee,
My Lady, Sweetie,
Sweet Mama,
Woman, Lovey, Bear,
Sweetheart, Minty,
Ma Bee Bee,
Darling, Bae,
She is a gift from God.
Bridge to bridge.
Border to border,
A warm blanket of love,
Life,
Created by God.
Your Momma!

Becoming Your Momma!

Her origin, source, and role resonate with people from all around the world culturally, traditionally, and spiritually. Her daily purpose is significant and woven within the structure of her family dynamic at all levels. As a matriarch and nurturer, she's the strength and backbone of the family. She creates the family legacy. She's a powerful rock, resilient, resourceful, loving, generous, kind, and often a good listener full of advice and wisdom. She has endearing names like Mimi, Mum, Mama, Mammy, Maem, Mom, Ma, Madee, My Lady, Sweetie, Sweet Mama, Ma Bee Bee, Nauna, Bae, and hundreds of other names globally expressed through various cultural lenses. Around the world, bridge to bridge, border to border, she creates a blanket of love that only God allows in Becoming Your Momma!

Mommas are often highly protected by their sons. Their daughters often lovingly walk in her shoes as mirror images. In a unified language across the globe, many people would agree it's not right to talk negatively about mommas. Whether momma jokes are meant as rib-cracking words expressed intentionally from the heart, or not. Simply, momma jokes are off limits. Truth be told, jokes about a person's momma often get under the skin of people. Spiritually, emotionally, morally, culturally, and even traditionally, when comedians, or people in general express jokes about mommas, the mother earth erupts, and an exchange of fighting words emerge. So, just don't go there. Simply, U-turn, and show total respect to Mommas!

Lady V Madisyn

Reflections

THE FABRIC OF AMERICA MUST COME TOGETHER

Unique.
Seeds.
You know it!
Where are we today?
2 thousand, what is the year?
You know it!
What's up?
Gas prices. Oh, no!
You know it!
What do we look like?
Church folk.
His Likeness.
Worldly.
Multi-faceted.
Whatever I want, that's how I feel,
I flow, now say it isn't so,
You know it!
Got needs,
Money,
Food,
Education,
Whatever!

Five fingers,
Now, get it.
You got it,
Go get it.
You know it!
Anybody hurt?
You know.
Who?
You know.
Who cares?
You said it.
No, you know it!
Where are we going?
Thriving and Surviving!
Legacy,
Now, got one.
You said it.
Okay,
What is the Fabric of America?
Culture, beliefs, values, the people.
Spiritual forces,
Grown-up Faith,
Who's good,
What's bad.

Talented,
Yes, and gifted,
Brilliant-Beautiful-Bold,
You know it!
Life is a Gift.
Free Will,
What's in your blueprint?
Life plan?
What is the Fabric of America?
People,
Woven Unity!
We are,
Who we are,
As we do,
What we do,
Make it count,
Live your worth.
Me,
You,
Us,
In His likeness,
Woven Unity.
The Fabric of America,
A collection of Unique Seeds!

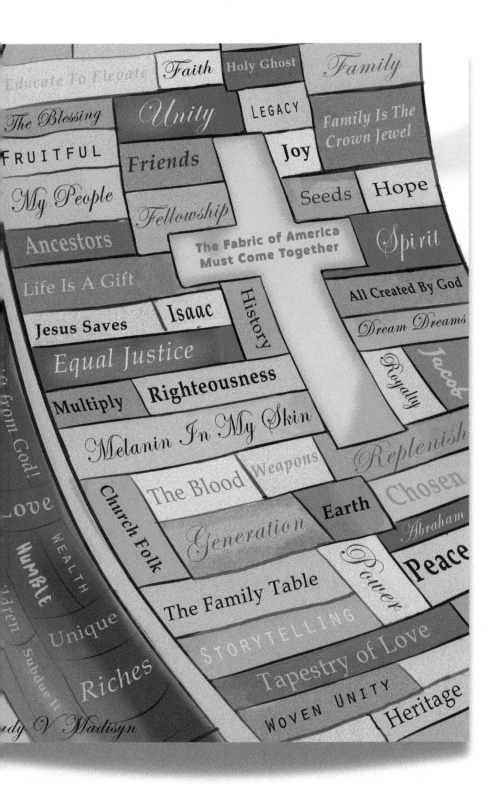

Reflections

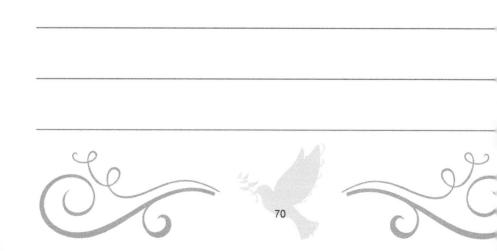

About the Author

Vanness D. Hughes (Lady V Madisyn) is a researcher and human services consultant, pursuing her doctoral degree in human and social services with a specialty in social policy, analysis, and planning. She obtained her Master of Social Work with a concentration in community organization and public policy from Howard University, her Master of Fine Arts in filmmaking from the New York Film Academy, and her Bachelor of Science in psychology with a minor in the Black Church from the University of Pittsburgh.

Lady V Madisyn also teaches screenwriting, film, and television media to adolescents and young adults. She enjoys serving as a film festival screener and screenplay reader. She is a member of The National Society of Leadership and Success, Women and Film, Delta Sigma Theta Sorority, Inc., serves as a director on the board of the Washington, D.C., Alumnae Foundation, and is a Christian servant leader helping youth and adults with their artistic creativity and spiritual development.

Learn more at www.belovellc.com

CPSIA information can be obtained
at www.ICGtesting.com
Printed in the USA
BVHW021238110921
616517BV00006B/603